Discovering Your Self-Worth: Understanding You Are Enough

By: Benedicta Olagbegi

Table of Content

Introduction

The journey towards self-discovery and self-acceptance can be a challenging one, but it is also a rewarding and transformative experience. In this book, "Discovering Your Self-Worth: Understanding You Are Enough," we explore the concept of self-worth and provide you with practical strategies for improving self-esteem and developing a positive sense of self.

Whether you struggle with low self-worth or simply want to live a more fulfilling life, this book is designed to help one understand the importance of self-worth and provide you with the tools needed to cultivate a strong and healthy sense of self. Through exploring your thoughts, emotions, values, and beliefs, this book provided information that can be used to embrace your authentic self and develop a strong foundation of self-worth and self-confidence.

With each chapter, we delve deeper into the various aspects of self-worth, including overcoming negative self-talk, embracing imperfections, practicing gratitude, and much more. The goal is to provide readers with a comprehensive guide to discovering their self-worth and live their best life. The book is filled with practical tips and advice for developing the skills and habits readers need to thrive. So, whether you're just starting your journey of self-discovery or looking to deepen your understanding of self-worth, this book is an excellent resource for anyone who wants to live a life that is fulfilling, meaningful, and satisfying. Let's begin!

Chapter 1

Introduction to Self-Worth

Self-worth is a complex and multi-faceted concept that has a profound impact on our lives. It is a fundamental aspect of our lives that influences our thoughts, feelings, and behaviors. Self-worth refers to the value we place on ourselves as individuals, and it shapes how we see ourselves including our relationships, experiences, and cultural influences, how we relate to others, and how we approach life. It can be both a source of strength and resilience, or a source of anxiety and self-doubt. Unfortunately, for many people, self-worth can be a difficult and elusive concept. We live in a world that often emphasizes perfection, success, and external validation, and it can be challenging to see our own worth when we are constantly bombarded with messages that tell us we need to do more, be more, and have more.

Despite its importance, self-worth is often neglected or overlooked in our fast-paced, achievement-driven society. We are bombarded with images and messages that tell us we are not good enough, that we need to be perfect, and that we need to achieve more in order to be successful and happy. These messages can be especially harmful to young people, who are in the process of developing their self-identity and self-worth. It is important to examine some of the factors that contribute to our self-worth and how these factors can be harnessed to support our growth and development.

What is Self-Worth?

Self-worth can be defined as the extent to which we believe in our own value and worth as a person. It reflects how we perceive ourselves and our sense of self-esteem. Our self-worth is not a fixed entity, but rather a dynamic and ever-changing aspect of our lives that can be influenced by a variety of internal and external factors. Most often, self-worth is thought of as being closely related to self-esteem, but there are some important differences between the two. While self-esteem refers to our overall evaluation of ourselves, self-worth refers to our sense of inherent worth and value as a person. It is not based on our achievements or external factors, but rather on our beliefs about ourselves and our worth as a person. In today's society self-worth is often taken for granted. Self-worth is the source of dignity and respect we give ourselves and is ultimately the first step to finding inner peace. Self-worth is tied to our self-esteem, and it is the belief we have in our own ability to do certain things and to bring value to the world.

The idea of being 'enough' can feel like a difficult concept to grasp, but that is because it requires both self-reflection and self-compassion. To discover your self-worth, you must work to recognize the unique strengths and talents you possess. Self-reflection includes the ability to recognize and accept your own strengths, weaknesses, successes, and failures, as well as being aware of your feelings, hopes, and dreams. When practiced regularly, self-reflection can be a powerful tool to help you identify your own worth.

The importance of self-compassion cannot be overlooked when it comes to discovering your self-worth either. It involves being kind and gentle to yourself even in the face of failure. Self-compassion is not the same as self-pity; it is the practice of being mindful of your own struggles and actively engaging with them to learn new ways to cope. It is essential because self-worth is derived from how much you are able to love and care for yourself from the inside out.

Why is Self-Worth Important?

Self-worth is critical to our well-being and overall happiness. When we have a strong sense of self-worth, we are more likely to feel confident, positive, and fulfilled. We are better able to navigate the challenges and obstacles of life and are less likely to be affected by negative thoughts and feelings. On the other hand, when we have a low sense of self-worth, we are more likely to experience anxiety, depression, and low self-esteem. We may also engage in self-sabotaging behaviors, such as substance abuse, eating disorders, or unhealthy relationships, that can further damage our self-worth and well-being.

It is important to note that self-worth is not the same as self-confidence. Self-confidence refers to our belief in our abilities and our trust in our judgment. While self-confidence can certainly contribute to our self-worth, it is not the same thing. A person with low self-worth may have high self-confidence in certain areas, but still struggle with feelings of insecurity and self-doubt.

Once you are more aware of your own personal strengths and weaknesses, you can start to appreciate yourself for all that you are and all that you have achieved. This sense of appreciation for yourself should be extended to your successes and achievements, but it should also be extended to your failures and mistakes. When you can do this, it will be much easier to accept and recognize your worth, as well as feeling more passionate about life and sharing your gifts with the world.

Factors that Contribute to Self-Worth

Self-worth is shaped by a variety of internal and external factors, including our relationships, experiences, and cultural influences. Some of the key factors that contribute to self-worth include:

- **Relationships:** Our relationships with family, friends, partners, and coworkers can have a significant impact on our self-worth. Positive relationships can provide us with support, validation, and a sense of belonging, which can boost our self-worth. Negative relationships, on the other hand, can be damaging and lead to feelings of insecurity and self-doubt.

- **Experiences:** Our experiences, both positive and negative, can also impact our self-worth. For example, experiencing success or recognition for our efforts can increase our sense of self-worth, while experiencing failure or criticism can be damaging.

- **Cultural influences:** The messages and beliefs of the culture in which we live can also play a role in shaping our self-worth. For example, some cultures emphasize individual achievement and success, while others emphasize the importance of community and relationships. These cultural messages can influence our beliefs about our own worth and value.

- **Trauma:** Traumatic experiences, such as abuse, neglect, or violence, can have a profound impact on our self-worth. These experiences can cause us to internalize negative messages and beliefs about ourselves, leading to low self-worth and a distorted sense of self.

- **Self-reflection:** Our own thoughts and beliefs about ourselves also play a critical role in shaping our self-worth. If we engage in negative self-talk or focus on our flaws and shortcomings, our self-worth will likely suffer. On the other hand, if we focus on our strengths and accomplishments and engage in positive self-talk, our self-worth will likely be strengthened.

The Importance of Nurturing Self-Worth

Given the critical role that self-worth plays in our lives, it is important that we make it a priority and invest in nurturing and strengthening it. This can be done through a variety of means, including:

- **Engaging in self-reflection:** By regularly taking time to reflect on our thoughts, feelings, and beliefs about ourselves, we can gain a deeper understanding of our self-worth and identify areas for growth and improvement.

- **Practicing self-care:** Taking care of ourselves, both physically and emotionally, is critical to maintaining and improving our self-worth. This includes engaging in activities that bring us joy, practicing mindfulness and relaxation techniques, and seeking out support when needed.

- **Seeking out positive relationships:** Surrounding ourselves with supportive and positive relationships can have a profound impact on our self-worth. This includes seeking out friends, family members, and coworkers who are supportive and validating, and avoiding those who are negative and critical.

- **Embracing failure and challenges:** Rather than viewing failure and challenges as evidence of our worthlessness, it is important that we view these experiences as opportunities for growth and learning. By embracing challenges and viewing failure as a necessary part of the process, we can strengthen our self-worth and resilience.

In conclusion, self-worth is a critical aspect of our lives that has a profound impact on our well-being and happiness.

Discovering your self-worth is not an easy task, but it will reap rewards in the long run. It requires regular self-reflection and self-compassion, as well as an appreciation for both your successes and your failures. It takes consistent effort to keep a positive mindset, practice positive self-talk, and seek support from those around you. With hard work and dedication, everyone can learn to value themselves for who they truly are and discover their own self-worth. By understanding the factors that contribute to self-worth and investing in nurturing and strengthening it, we can build a life filled with confidence, positivity, and fulfillment.

Chapter 2

Understanding Your Thoughts and Emotions

The relationship between our thoughts, emotions, and self-worth is complex and interdependent. Our thoughts and emotions have a significant impact on our self-worth, and conversely, our self-worth influences our thoughts and emotions. In order to build and maintain a healthy self-worth, it is important to understand how our thoughts and emotions shape our self-perception and to learn techniques for managing and regulating them. This knowledge is beneficial because it helps to inform you of how you interact with the world and others around you, making your life much more manageable and meaningful. Taking the time to familiarize ourselves with our emotions and thoughts can lead to improved sense of self-worth and secure our belief in who we are and what we stand for.

In order to understand and nurture our self-worth, it is critical that we become aware of and take control of our thoughts and emotions. Our thoughts and emotions play a central role in shaping our self-worth, and by understanding how they work and how they impact our lives, we can develop the skills and strategies needed to build a strong sense of self-worth.

The Power of Thoughts

Our thoughts play a critical role in shaping our self-worth. The way we think about ourselves, others, and the world around us shapes our perceptions and beliefs about our own worth and value. This, in turn, influences our emotions and behaviors.

For example, if we engage in negative self-talk, such as calling ourselves names or focusing on our flaws, we will likely feel insecure and have a low sense of self-worth. On the other hand, if we focus on our strengths and accomplishments and engage in positive self-talk, our self-worth will likely be stronger. It is important to be mindful of our thoughts and to engage in regular self-reflection to identify patterns of negative self-talk. Once we are aware of these patterns, we can work to replace them with more positive, affirming thoughts. This can be done through a variety of means, including journaling, meditation, and visualization exercises.

When you take the time to understand your thoughts and emotions, you are able to recognize your personal strength and be comfortable with who you are. You can identify when you may be overthinking or worrying too much and have the capability to connect more accurately what you are feeling with your reactions and behaviors. This understanding provides you with the tools to give yourself compassion and also learn how to choose better-aligned thoughts and emotions that can help you move forward in a positive direction.

The Connection Between Thoughts and Emotions

Our thoughts and emotions are closely interconnected, and each can have a powerful impact on the other. For example, if we have negative thoughts about ourselves, such as "I'm not good enough," these thoughts can lead to feelings of sadness, anxiety, or frustration. Conversely, if we have positive thoughts about ourselves, such as "I am capable and competent," these thoughts can lead to feelings of confidence and happiness. Given this close connection between thoughts and emotions, it is important that we become more mindful of our thoughts and the impact they have on our lives. This can be done by engaging in regular self-reflection and examining the thoughts and beliefs we hold about ourselves.

Identifying Negative Thoughts and Beliefs

One of the first steps in taking control of our thoughts and emotions is to identify any negative or harmful thoughts and beliefs we may have about ourselves. These negative thoughts and beliefs can be deeply ingrained and may have been developed over many years, but they are not necessarily accurate or reflective of who we truly are.

Some common negative thoughts and beliefs that can impact our self-worth include:

- I'm not good enough.
- I'm not smart enough.
- I'm not attractive enough.
- I'm not successful enough.
- I'm not loved or accepted.

Managing Negative Thoughts

Negative thoughts can have a profound impact on our self-worth, leading to feelings of insecurity and self-doubt. To manage negative thoughts, it is important to engage in critical thinking, so that we can evaluate the accuracy of these thoughts and challenge them.

For example, if we have the thought that we are not good enough, we can engage in critical thinking by asking ourselves:

- Is this thought based on evidence or is it just a negative assumption?
- What is the evidence to support this thought?
- What is the evidence against this thought?

Once we have identified these negative thoughts and beliefs, it is important that we challenge them and work to replace them with more positive and accurate beliefs. This can be done through a variety of means, including therapy, self-reflection, and positive self-talk.

Alongside identifying and analyzing your thoughts and emotions, it is also essential to recognize that you are enough. It is essential to remember to be kind to yourself and recognize that you do not have to be a certain way or achieve specific goals to be worthy of love. This understanding allows you to be gentler with yourself and know that the traits which make you unique are enough, or that mistakes are mere steppingstones along your path rather than roadblocks.

The Power of Positive Self-Talk

Positive self-talk is an effective tool for nurturing our self-worth and improving our well-being. By speaking kindly and positively to ourselves, we can counteract negative thoughts and beliefs and promote feelings of self-acceptance and self-love.

Some strategies for using positive self-talk to improve our self-worth include:

- **Reframing negative thoughts:** When we have negative thoughts, it is important that we reframe them in a more positive and accurate light. For example, instead of thinking "I'm not good enough," we can think "I am capable and competent, and I will continue to grow and improve."

- **Engaging in positive affirmations:** Positive affirmations are short, positive statements that we repeat to ourselves as a means of promoting positive thoughts and beliefs. Some examples of positive affirmations include "I am worthy and deserving of love and happiness," and "I am capable and competent, and I am making a positive difference in the world."

- **Practicing gratitude:** Practicing gratitude by focusing on the things we are thankful for can help shift our focus from negative thoughts to positive ones. By focusing on the good in our lives, we can promote feelings of gratitude and contentment, and improve our self-worth.

The Importance of Emotional Regulation

Emotional regulation refers to the process of managing and regulating our emotions, so that they do not become overwhelming or interfere with our daily lives. Emotional regulation is critical to maintaining and improving our self-worth, as negative emotions such as anger, sadness, or anxiety can lead to negative thoughts and beliefs about ourselves.

There are several strategies that can be used to regulate emotions, including:

- **Mindfulness:** Mindfulness involves paying attention to the present moment and our thoughts and emotions without judgment. By practicing mindfulness, we can gain a better understanding of our emotions and learn to regulate them.

- **Deep breathing:** Deep breathing is a simple but effective technique for managing emotions. By taking slow, deep breaths, we can calm our bodies and reduce the intensity of our emotions.

- **Exercise:** Exercise has been shown to have a positive impact on our emotions, reducing symptoms of stress and anxiety and improving our overall well-being.

- **Seek support:** Seeking support from family members, friends, or mental health professionals can be an effective way to regulate emotions. Talking through our feelings with others can help us gain a new perspective and learn new strategies for managing our emotions and nurture self-worth.

The Role of Emotions in Nurturing Self-Worth

In addition to thoughts, our emotions also play a critical role in shaping our self-worth. Our emotions are the body's way of communicating information about our experiences and provide valuable information about our needs and desires, but they can also be overwhelming and difficult to manage.

For example, if we feel sad, angry, or frustrated, it may be a sign that we need to address an underlying issue or situation. These emotions can also have a negative impact on our self-worth, leading us to feel insecure or inadequate. It is important to learn techniques for managing and regulating our emotions, such as mindfulness, deep breathing, and cognitive-behavioral therapy. By developing the skills to manage our emotions, we can prevent them from overwhelming us and negatively impacting our self-worth.

By engaging in critical thinking and evaluating the accuracy of our thoughts, we can learn to challenge negative thinking patterns and replace them with more positive and accurate thoughts. Learning these skills also benefits your relationships with others and able to comprehend interpersonal cues and helps you create more meaningful and deep connections. This also allows you to help others work through difficult situation and to build stronger relationships with those around you. Due to the enhanced understanding, each conversation is more enriched as both parties are able to connect and come to more meaningful conclusions.

In conclusion, our thoughts and emotions play a critical role in shaping our self-worth, and understanding the relationship between these two elements is essential to nurturing our self-worth. Being able to recognize your thoughts and emotions, while understanding that you are enough are both important skills to have. Becoming more aware of your own thought patterns, feelings and actions can not only help you be fair to yourself but to also create more meaningful connections with others. Being mindful of this knowledge will help you to feel more comfortable in your own skin, own yourself and believe that you are enough. By managing and regulating our emotions and engaging in critical thinking, we can learn to manage our negative thoughts.

Chapter 3

Exploring Your Values and Beliefs

Our identity is comprised of the beliefs, values, and decisions we make in our lives. On this journey of self-discovery, it is important to take time to reflect on who you are and what you stand for. Our values and beliefs are critical to our self-worth, as they shape our perceptions of ourselves and the world around us. In this chapter, we will explore the role that our values and beliefs play in shaping our self-worth, and the steps we can take to better understand and align our values and beliefs with our goals and aspirations.

What are Values and Beliefs?

Values are the principles or standards that guide our actions and decisions. They are the things that we hold dear and that are important to us, such as honesty, kindness, and compassion. Our values serve as the foundation for our beliefs and beliefs are the convictions or opinions that we hold about ourselves, others, and the world.

The Role of Values and Beliefs in Shaping Our Self-Worth

Our values and beliefs have a significant impact on our self-worth, as they shape our perceptions of ourselves and the world around us. For example, if we have the belief that success is the most important thing in life, this belief can shape our perceptions of our own worth, causing us to feel inadequate if we are not successful. Similarly, if we hold values such as honesty and integrity, these values can shape our perceptions of ourselves, causing us to feel good about ourselves when we act in accordance with these values.

Exploring Your Values and Beliefs

Exploring your values and beliefs is a key component of understanding you and paving the way for an authentic and fulfilling life. When you know what values are important to you, and what beliefs you hold, you become better equipped to make decisions that align with who you are. Some of the values and beliefs that may be important to you include integrity, honesty, kindness, respect, humility, family, and equality. These are simply examples that may or may not be relevant or important to you, as everyone's values are unique.

To better understand your values and beliefs, it is important to engage in self-reflection and introspection. This can involve asking yourself questions such as:

- What are the things that are important to me?
- What do I believe about myself and the world around me?
- How do my beliefs and values shape my perceptions of myself and my self-worth?

You can also use journaling, meditating, or speaking with a trusted friend or family member to explore your values and beliefs. By exploring your values and beliefs, you can gain a better understanding of what is important to you and what shapes your perceptions of yourself and the world around you. It is important to remember that whatever values and beliefs you come up with, the most important one of all is self-love and self-acceptance. Having true self-worth and believing that you are, and always will be, enough is invaluable and something to strive towards.

Aligning Your Values and Beliefs with Your Goals and Aspirations

Once you have explored your values and beliefs, it is important to align them with your goals and aspirations. This involves evaluating whether your values and beliefs are in line with what you want to achieve in life and whether they are helping or hindering your progress. For example, if you have the belief that success is the most important thing in life, but you also value honesty and integrity, it is important to determine whether this belief is aligned with your goals and aspirations. If it is not, you may need to re-evaluate your beliefs and find ways to align them with your values.

When it comes to knowing thyself, if we are able to identify our traits, characteristics, and values then who are we not to trust and believe in ourselves? Knowing that you have the power to make decisions which honor who you are is empowering. If your values and beliefs are not aligned with your goals and aspirations, you may need to make changes to your beliefs and values. This can involve finding new beliefs and values that align with your goals and aspirations, or developing a new perspective on the beliefs and values that you already hold.

The Importance of Authenticity

It is important to align your values and beliefs with your goals and aspirations, but it is equally important to remain authentic and true to yourself. This means that you should not try to adopt values and beliefs that are not truly important to you or that do not align with your authentic self. By staying true to yourself and aligning your values and beliefs with your goals and aspirations, you can increase your self-worth and lead a life that is fulfilling and meaningful. A strong sense of self-worth can bring greater happiness, fulfillment, and success in all areas of life.

Accepting yourself fully and being comfortable in your individuality means that being 'enough' is not only achievable, but it is something to strive for and something to celebrate. Strength comes when we are able to effectively express ourselves, stand up for our beliefs and bring our best self to every situation we encounter. You can create the life you want when you truly believe in yourself, and when you accept and honor who you are.

As you continue this journey, keep in mind that it's okay to make mistakes and to stumble along the way. The most important thing is to keep moving forward and to never give up on yourself. Remember, you are worthy of love, happiness, and success, and by exploring and aligning your values and beliefs, you can bring these things into your life.

In conclusion, our values and beliefs play a critical role in shaping our self-worth, and exploring and aligning these elements is essential to nurturing our self-worth. By engaging in self-reflection and introspection, and by aligning our values and beliefs with our goals and aspirations, we can develop a strong sense of self-worth and lead a fulfilling and meaningful life. Exploring, accepting, and embracing your values and beliefs is a journey that will help shape who you are, and it is a journey worth taking. The ability to love and trust yourself is something we can all strive for, but you must understand, appreciate, and honor yourself first. So, take some time to reflect on your values and beliefs and to consider how they shape your perceptions of yourself and the world around you. Remember, your self-worth is an important aspect of your life, and by exploring and aligning your values and beliefs, you can strengthen your self-worth and lead a more fulfilling life and know that you are enough.

Chapter 4

Overcoming Negative Self-Talk

Negative self-talk is a common and harmful aspect of many people's lives. It can take many forms, such as criticizing ourselves, making comparisons with others, or doubting our abilities. Negative self-talk can be debilitating, leading to feelings of low self-esteem, anxiety, and depression. It can seem like there's no way to just shut off your negative thoughts and zero in on the positives. But it's important to realize that negative self-talk can be addressed and conquered. The good news is that negative self-talk can be overcome, and with practice and persistence, it is possible to transform negative self-talk into positive, supportive thoughts.

The first step in overcoming negative self-talk is to recognize it. This means developing an awareness of when and how those negative thoughts creep into your head. It can feel like it's impossible to control the thoughts going through your mind, but it's important to stay mindful of your inner narrative so that you can reach out to it and bring it back to more healthy, realistic thought patterns. Paying attention to your thoughts and noticing when you engage in negative self-talk. Once you have become aware of your negative self-talk, you can begin to challenge and change it. It's important to keep in mind that changing negative self-talk takes time and practice. It's not something that will happen overnight, but with persistence, it is possible to overcome negative self-talk and to transform it into positive, supportive thoughts.

One way to challenge negative self-talk is to question its validity and reframing your thoughts. Ask yourself, "Is this thought really true?" "Is there any evidence to support this thought?" Often, we find that our negative self-talk is based on false or distorted beliefs, and by questioning its validity, we can begin to see our thoughts and ourselves in a more positive light.

Another way to challenge negative self-talk is to replace it with positive affirmations. This means actively seeking out and repeating positive, supportive thoughts to counteract the negative self-talk. For example, if you find yourself thinking "I'm not good enough," you can replace that thought with "I am capable and competent." remind yourself that you are good enough and focus on the little victories in your day. Negative thoughts come in all shapes and sizes, but know that no matter how angry, dark, or negative they may seem at first, there's a way to look at the situation in a kinder and more understanding light.

Other ways include Practice mindfulness: Mindfulness is the practice of being present in the moment and paying attention to your thoughts, feelings, and sensations. By practicing mindfulness, you can become more aware of your negative self-talk and be better equipped to challenge and change it.

Another way is to surround yourself with positive people: Surrounding yourself with positive people can help to counteract negative self-talk. Surround yourself with people who support and encourage you, and who believe in you and your abilities. You may also find it helpful to talk with a close friend or family member about the negative thinking and feeling of worthlessness that comes with negative self-talk. This can be incredibly validating and can bring a sense of comfort and perspective to the situation. It's also important to be kind to yourself as there's no need to put yourself down for having these types of thoughts. Other ways include:

Engage in physical activity: Engaging in physical activity, such as exercise, can help to reduce stress, increase feelings of well-being, and counteract negative self-talk. When we feel good physically, it can be easier to think more positively.

Write down your negative self-talk: Writing down your negative self-talk can help you to become more aware of it, and better equipped to challenge and change it. Write down the negative thoughts, past mistakes, and feelings you experience, and then challenge each one by asking yourself, "Is this thought really true?" "Is there any evidence to support this thought?" We all make mistakes, and it's important to forgive ourselves and move on. Take this time to look at how you can improve in the future and recognize your successes. Do what it takes to remind yourself that you are enough.

Focus on your strengths: Focusing on your strengths and accomplishments can help to counteract negative self-talk. Make a list of your strengths and refer to it whenever you experience negative self-talk. This will help you to see yourself in a more positive light.

Seek professional help: If negative self-talk is affecting your life in a significant way, it may be helpful to seek professional help. A therapist or counselor can help you to understand and challenge negative self-talk and provide you with tools and strategies to overcome it.

Self-compassion: To changing negative self-talk, it's also important to practice self-compassion. This involves being kind and understanding towards yourself and recognizing that everyone makes mistakes and experiences challenges. By being self-compassionate, you can reduce feelings of self-criticism and increase feelings of self-worth. It is also important to engage in activities that promote self-reflection and self-awareness. This can include journaling, meditation, or therapy. By exploring our thoughts and emotions, we can better understand and challenge negative self-talk, and increase our self-worth.

In conclusion, negative self-talk is a common and harmful aspect of many people's lives, but it can be overcome. By becoming aware of negative self-talk, challenging its validity, replacing it with positive affirmations, practicing self-compassion, and engaging in activities that promote self-reflection and self-awareness, it is possible to transform negative self-talk into positive, supportive thoughts and increase self-worth. Overcoming negative self-talk is a journey, and it takes time and practice, and it is not something you have to live with forever. Taking steps towards understanding and addressing it can give you the strength and resilience to conquer your negative inner dialogue. So be patient with yourself, and never give up. You are worthy of love, happiness, and success, and with persistence, you can overcome negative self-talk and bring these things into your life. You are enough and there are ways to quiet that inner negative self-talk and get back to feeling your best.

Chapter 5

Learning to Accept and Love Yourself

Self-love is the foundation of self-worth, and learning to accept and love yourself is an essential step in the journey towards a healthier and happier life. Learning to accept and love yourself is one of the most important aspects of achieving true inner peace. The truth is that you are enough exactly as you are in this moment. No matter what insecurities, doubts or fears preoccupy you, it is essential to recognize that you have worth and value.

Self-love can start with small changes to your daily routine. Make sure to give yourself time and space to disconnect from the digital world and its distracting demands. It is important to take a break from people and to create moments in your day to simply be with yourself. Practice self-care by engaging in activities that bring you joy. Pamper yourself, focus on doing the things you enjoy, and your sense of worth will grow. Additionally, do something that challenges you. Find an activity that encourages growth and self-discovery. Anything from volleyball to reading; setting a goal and reaching it can be a powerful validation of your capabilities.

It is important to try to look for the positive side of every situation and be kind to yourself. However, do not get so caught up in positive thinking that you don't allow yourself to feel sadness or anger, for these are important emotions too. Both positive and negative lessons can be learned from the events of life, and it is up to you to decide how you cope with them.

Know and acknowledge your flaws, but don't dwell on them. Everyone has different strengths and weaknesses, and that's okay. Surround yourself with relationships that are built on mutual respect and love. Also, practice kindness and open-mindedness towards others. Compliment yourself and others. Make room for creativity, practice expressing yourself whether it is through art, Instagram, YouTube, writing - any way that works for you. Constantly remind yourself "You are enough." Self-love is about recognizing your own worth and value, and treating yourself with kindness, compassion, and respect.

Steps to Accept and Love Yourself

- One of the first steps in learning to accept and love yourself is to understand that you are enough just as you are. You don't need to change yourself to be accepted or loved. You are worthy of love and respect simply because you exist.

- Another important step in learning to love yourself is to be kind to yourself. Treat yourself the way you would treat a good friend. When you make a mistake, be gentle with yourself. Instead of criticizing or berating yourself, offer yourself compassion and understanding.

- It's also important to take care of your physical and emotional needs. This includes things like eating well, getting enough sleep, and engaging in physical activity. By taking care of yourself, you are sending a message to yourself that you are worthy of love and respect.

- One of the keys to self-love is to focus on your positive qualities and accomplishments. Make a list of the things you like about yourself and refer to it whenever you need a boost of confidence. This will help you to see yourself in a more positive light, and to appreciate the unique and wonderful person you are.

- Another way to increase self-love is to surround yourself with positive and supportive people. Seek out people who love and accept you for who you are, and who support your goals and aspirations. Surrounding yourself with positive people will help you to feel better about yourself, and to develop a more positive self-image.

- Finally, learning to accept and love yourself also involves developing a healthy self-image. This means recognizing your own value and worth and seeing yourself as a valuable and deserving person. A healthy self-image will help you to feel more confident and secure in your own skin, and to better navigate the challenges of life.

- Above all, maintain an attitude of gratitude. As hard as it may be to do at times, be grateful for everything and everyone in your life. Understand that everything in life is a learning experience, and no setback or failure can change the value you hold. Life is short and it is important to make the most of each day by living in the present moment. Through recognition of your worth, practice of self-care and gratitude, and an attitude of open-mindedness and kindness, true self-love and immense self-value can be achieved.

In conclusion, learning to accept and love yourself is a journey, and it may take time and effort. But by being patient and persistent, and by using the tips and strategies outlined in this chapter, you can develop a stronger and more positive sense of self-worth and increase your self-love and self-acceptance.

Chapter 6

Building Confidence

Confidence is an essential component of self-worth and is closely related to self-love and self-acceptance. Confidence is about believing in yourself, your abilities, and your worth as a person. When you have confidence, you are more likely to take risks, pursue your goals, and live your life to the fullest. When it comes to building confidence, many people believe that it can be achieved through material accomplishments, career success, and physical beauty. However, these are all external qualities and sources of confidence. The most important factor in building self-confidence is discovering an internal sense of worth and realizing that you are enough, just the way you are. And confidence is built with a defined self-esteem.

Self-esteem can be thought of as a positive or negative opinion we have of ourselves, while self-confidence is closely related to self-esteem and involves the belief in our abilities, values, and assets. It is also rooted in the development of self-trust and the belief that overall; you are a worthy and valuable person. A good self-esteem builds self confidence that enables you to react with courage to life's challenges.

Ways to Build Self-Confidence

One of the best ways to start building your confidence is by understanding yourself and learning to recognize and challenge negative self-talk. Have a shift in mindset and challenge negative beliefs and false assumptions you may have about yourself. Taking a step back to examine faulty though processes can be a difficult but valuable step that can help you to question harmful thought patterns and see yourself more objectively. This means paying attention to the thoughts and beliefs that hold you back, and learning to replace them with positive, empowering thoughts. To do this, it is important to look at why you feel lacking in confidence and identify the areas in your life that are causing this. Once these are identified, it is important to focus on shifting your mindset and internal dialogue. Make effort to be kind and gentle to yourself, even if this may feel unnatural.

Practicing resilience is another way to build self-confidence when you look for ways to pick yourself up whenever obstacles arise. Learning to embrace failure and using it as a learning opportunity is an important part of developing confidence. Practicing resilience helps one to develop the ability to bounce back from challenges and setbacks. When we are resilient, we are better equipped to handle obstacles and challenges, and we don't let setbacks define us or hold us back. This ability to face challenges with determination and grit can build our confidence and self-esteem, as we see that we are capable of handling difficult situations and that we have the strength and resilience to overcome them.

Another effective way to build confidence is to set and achieve small goals. Start by setting achievable goals that are aligned with your values and aspirations, and then work towards achieving them. Each time you reach a goal, no matter how small, you will build your confidence and increase your self-worth. It is also important to practice self-compassion. Celebrate your strengths and successes and acknowledge any progress you make when working towards your goals. This can help to create a greater feeling of self-worth, which is essential in building self-confidence.

Developing positive self-image is another way to build confidence. A positive self-image is the way you see and think about yourself, and it includes your beliefs, attitudes, and opinions about yourself and your abilities. When you have a positive self-image, you view yourself as worthy, capable, and deserving of respect and success. Having a positive self-image can help you feel more confident in your abilities and less self-conscious in social situations. You are more likely to trust yourself, take risks, and pursue your goals and aspirations when you have a positive view of yourself. In addition, a positive self-image can also help you better handle criticism and rejections, as you are less likely to take these experiences personally or as reflections of your worth. This means focusing on your strengths and positive qualities and working to develop a positive and accurate self-perception. A positive self-image will help you to feel better about yourself and to be more confident in your interactions with others.

Confidence can also be built through self-care practices. This includes taking care of your physical and emotional needs, such as getting enough sleep, eating well, and engaging in physical activity. By taking care of yourself, you are sending a message to yourself that you are worthy of love and respect, and that you are capable of taking care of your own needs.

Surrounding yourself with positive and supportive people is also an important factor in building confidence. Seek out people who encourage and support you, and who help you to see the best in yourself. Having a strong support system can help you to feel more confident and secure, and to better navigate the challenges of life.

It's also important to practice self-compassion. This means being kind and gentle with yourself, and treating yourself with the same kindness and compassion that you would offer to a good friend. When you practice self-compassion, you are more likely to develop a positive self-image and to increase your self-worth.

Finally, confidence can be developed through mindfulness and meditation practices. Mindfulness helps you to be more present and aware in the moment, and to develop a deeper understanding of your thoughts, feelings, and emotions. Meditation can help you to develop a sense of inner peace and calm, and to increase your confidence and self-worth.

Obstacles to Building Confidence

From a young age, humans are tempted to seek the approval of their peers, usually as a way to fit in with popular trends and social circles. This can be seen in how children will mimic their family and peers in order to earn respect, or how teenagers will follow fellow students in order to belong to certain "cliques." Even as adults, many people find it necessary to please their bosses in order to gain monetary rewards, or to impress colleagues to expand their professional network. Unfortunately, in the process of seeking approval, people often sacrifice their own interests, opinions, and opinions in order to please others. This can be a detriment to oneself as it can lead to low self-confidence and feeling unworthy or unimportant. Unfortunately, there are many obstacles of seeking approval from others in order to build self-confidence.

One of the biggest obstacles to building confidence is seeking approval from others. Many people believe that they can only feel good about themselves if they receive validation and recognition from others. They may constantly seek approval from friends, family, or even strangers, hoping to feel more confident and secure. For example, when a person is constantly trying to meet the expectations of others just to belong and to make society see them as one of the elites or a top socialite, with time, they feel trapped between multiple windows of approval and soon, they begin to blur the line between opinions and desires. This confusion can lead to insecurity and doubt because it can be challenging to assess whether one's decisions are truly in line with what they personally value rather than the opinions of others. As a result, they can struggle to make wise decisions on their own and feel overwhelmed and defeated in the process. However, seeking approval from others is an ineffective way to build confidence because it places your sense of self-worth in the hands of others. When your self-worth is based on external validation, you become vulnerable to criticism, rejection, and disappointment.

Another issue that can hinder confidence is associating with people just because they are wealthy, have a big house, expensive cars, or impressive career. While these people may seem confident and successful on the surface, they may not be good role models for building confidence. Associating with people who are overly focused on external success and material possessions can create a sense of insecurity and comparison. You may start to feel that you are not good enough or that you don't measure up. This can lead to a decrease in your self-worth and confidence.

Instead of seeking approval from others or associating with people who are focused on external success, focus on building confidence from within. This means developing a strong sense of self-worth and self-acceptance that is based on your own values, beliefs, and achievements. Start by setting and achieving your own goals and focusing on your own personal growth and development. Surround yourself with positive, supportive people who encourage and empower you, and who help you to see the best in yourself.

Focus on your strengths and positive qualities, and practice self-compassion and self-care. Seek out new experiences and challenges that help you to develop new skills and to grow as a person. Remember that confidence is not about external validation or material possessions, but about believing in yourself, your abilities, and your worth as a person. When you focus on building confidence from within, you are more likely to feel confident, secure, and happy, no matter what others may think or say.

Seeking approval from others and associating with people who are focused on external success and material possessions can be detrimental to your confidence and self-worth. Instead, focus on building confidence from within by setting and achieving your own goals, surrounding yourself with positive and supportive people, focusing on your strengths, and practicing self-compassion and self-care.

In conclusion, building confidence is an important step in the journey towards a healthier and happier life. By learning to recognize and challenge negative self-talk, setting and achieving small goals, developing a positive self-image, taking care of your physical and emotional needs, surrounding yourself with positive people, practicing self-compassion, and engaging in mindfulness and meditation practices, you can develop a stronger and more confident sense of self-worth. Building confidence is a life-long process. Discovering that you are enough and having an internal sense of worth is essential to this process, as this will lay the foundation for building a strong sense of self-esteem and self-confidence that can carry you forward in times of difficulty and challenge.

Chapter 7

Finding Your Purpose

Finding your purpose in life can be a challenging journey, but it is also one of the most rewarding. Your purpose is the reason for which you were put on this earth, and it is what gives your life meaning and fulfillment. For many people, finding their purpose takes time, introspection, and exploration. It can be helpful to start by reflecting on your values, beliefs, and interests. What are the things that matter most to you? What are you passionate about? What makes you feel alive and energized? Once you have a better understanding of your values, beliefs, and interests, you can start exploring different paths that align with your purpose. This might involve volunteering, trying new hobbies, or taking courses in areas that interest you.

The journey of self-discovery and finding your purpose in life is not easy. It takes time and patience, especially when you have doubts or feel stuck. When this happens, remember that you are enough. It's important to keep in mind that your purpose may evolve over time. What matters to you now may change as you grow and mature. Don't be afraid to try new things and explore different avenues until you find what truly resonates with you.

In addition to exploring your passions, it's also helpful to seek out mentors, role models, and people who have found their purpose in life. They can offer valuable advice, support, and guidance as you navigate your own journey. Talk to a trusted friend or mentor who can help you reflect on your values, put them into action, and move forward. It is also important to maintain your mental and physical health. This involves eating well, staying active, and taking time for yourself. Do activities that you enjoy and make you feel alive.

Another key component of finding your purpose is service to others. Many people find that serving others, either through volunteer work or by helping friends and family, is incredibly fulfilling. It can provide a sense of meaning and purpose and help to put things into perspective. It is also important to have the willingness to take risks in the journey of discovering your purpose in life. This can involve pursuing opportunities, leaving a current job, or joining a new organization. Believe in yourself, and don't be afraid to fail. You will both succeed and fail at different points in your life, and the key is to learn from each experience.

It is also important that you evaluate the successes and failures and use them as opportunities to make changes and keep heading in the right direction. As you work to find your purpose, it's important to be patient and kind to yourself. This can be a challenging journey, and it may take some time to find your way. But with persistence, introspection, and a willingness to explore new avenues, you will eventually find your purpose and the fulfillment that comes with it.

In conclusion, finding your purpose in life can be a journey of discovery, exploration, and growth. Start by reflecting on your values, beliefs, and interests, and seek out opportunities to explore new avenues that align with your purpose. Seek out mentors and role models, and don't be afraid to try new things. Ultimately, when you accept that you are enough, you can build on your skills and begin to shape your life to be purposeful and fulfilling. Keep reflecting on what goals you want to achieve and how your values can manifest into tangible actions. Believe in yourself and the power of self-improvement, and you will be able to reach your purpose. With patience, persistence, and a willingness to grow, you will eventually find your purpose and the fulfillment that comes with it.

Chapter 8

Setting Boundaries

It is essential to have boundaries when discovering yourself and coming to terms with who you are. Boundaries help to define who you are, what you stand for, and what is and isn't acceptable in your relationships and interactions with others. After all, true self-discovery involves significant introspection and the development of healthy self-esteem and a sense of personal worth.

To achieve this propitious state in the most beneficial manner, boundaries must be considered. However, setting boundaries can be difficult, especially if you've been taught to prioritize other people's needs over your own. It can be tempting to put others first, but it's important to remember that taking care of yourself is essential to your well-being. Having knowledge of and setting your personal boundaries is an important part of journey towards self-discovery.

Steps to Set Boundaries

The first step in setting boundaries is to understand your own values and beliefs. What do you stand for? What are your non-negotiables? Knowing what you value and believe in will help you to establish clear and healthy boundaries in your relationships and interactions with others. Creating boundaries begins with understanding what you are and are not comfortable with regarding how you interact with the world and the people around you. It's a process of owning your feelings, honoring your emotions, and validating your experiences. Acknowledging the want for a boundary is the starting point, followed by creating standards to maintain that boundary.

Next, it's important to be honest and direct with others about your boundaries. Communicate your needs and wants, and let others know what is and isn't okay in your relationship with them. By establishing boundaries, you can determine what influences you honor or reject as well as determine how you want others to treat you. Having well-defined boundaries lets you know you are strong in your convictions no matter your relationship status, job, or financial situation. Make sure to be clear, concise, and firm, and remember that it's okay to say no.

In some cases, setting boundaries may mean ending toxic relationships or walking away from people or situations that are harmful to your well-being. This can be difficult, but it's important to remember that you deserve to be treated with respect and dignity and you do not always have to be surrounded by drama and unnecessary fights. As you end toxic relationship, it is important that you respect others' boundaries and be mindful of their needs and wants. This means avoiding imposing your own beliefs and values on others and recognizing that what is important to you may not be important to someone else.

In establishing boundaries, maintain healthy boundaries, it's also important to practice self-care. It is also essential to remember to be gentle with yourself. It is not selfish or wrong to prioritize your own well-being, to take time to rest and to be kind to your own soul. Taking care of yourself and honoring your boundaries is a part of being enough. This means taking time for yourself, engaging in activities that bring you joy and fulfillment, and making time for self-reflection and introspection.

Self-love is not limited to what you can do for yourself; it's also about recognizing when it's time to take a step back and stop trying to please the world. Setting boundaries will help you in turn to broaden your focus and give you the space to determine who you are and what truly matters to you.

Finally, Creating, and nurturing boundaries for yourself is key to ensure that you practice self-love and respect, enabling your life to be successful both personally and professionally. The truth is that it's not simply about establishing boundaries but honoring those boundaries. Focusing on those boundaries is a commitment to the awareness of patterns in your external and internal world, recognizing what is healthy for or unhealthy for you and developing the strength to take genuine action. Be patient with yourself and others as you work to establish healthy boundaries. It may take time and practice, but with persistence and a commitment to your well-being, you will be able to create healthy, meaningful relationships and interactions with others.

In conclusion, setting boundaries is an essential part of living a fulfilling life. By understanding your own values and beliefs, being honest and direct with others, and practicing self-care, you can establish healthy, meaningful relationships and interactions with others. With healthy boundaries and genuine understanding of yourself and motivations to discover your truth, it is possible to find the courage to be enough and you can build the kind of life that you want and deserve.

Chapter 9

Letting Go of Perfectionism

As one begins to explore and discover yourself and finding your identity, it is essential for them to be aware of the dangers of perfectionism. Perfectionism is a way of thinking that establishes unrealistic expectations for oneself and can lead to lasting feelings of fear, frustration, and disappointment. Although striving for excellence can be beneficial and is certainly to be encouraged, the pressure of perfectionism can lead to the antithesis of personal growth; the feeling of being completely overwhelmed and unable to progress.

The idea that one must be perfect to be accepted or be considered successful is damaging and can cause an individual to feel completely discouraged and insecure. As such, it is important that when exploring one's identity they begin to accept flaws and imperfections and understand that they are enough as they are.

Perfectionism can be a major roadblock in our journey towards self-worth and self-acceptance. We often believe that to be accepted and loved, we have to be perfect in all aspects of our lives, from our appearance to our careers to our relationships. This can lead to feelings of constant self-doubt and inadequacy and can make it difficult to find joy and fulfillment in our lives.

The notion that an individual needs to attain a certain level of perfection before they can be accepted is sadly a widespread one. Many people, particularly those who follow the teachings of perfectionism, have come to conceive mistakes and imperfections as a weakness, a sign that they are inadequate. Those who possess this view believe that to be admired, accepted, and be seen as successful, they must strive to live up to unrealistic expectations both of themselves and of others.

Unfortunately, this idea of perfectionism works in direct opposition to priority of personal growth and exploration, instead leading to the consumption of energy and focus that could be used to further oneself. As such, it is important to recognize the notion of perfectionism when it sprawls up, acknowledge it as an obstacle, and begin to overcome it on one's own terms.

Steps to Prevent Perfectionism

The first step in letting go of perfectionism is to understand where it comes from. Perfectionism is often rooted in childhood experiences or cultural messages that tell us that we must be perfect to be loved and accepted. It can also stem from a fear of failure or a desire for control.

Next, it's important to challenge these perfectionist beliefs and thoughts. This means recognizing when you're being overly critical of yourself and others and trying to replace these thoughts with more positive, self-compassionate ones. This can be difficult, but with practice, it will become easier over time.

Another important step in letting go of perfectionism is to embrace your flaws and imperfections. This means accepting that you are human, and that it's okay to make mistakes. Try to view your imperfections as opportunities for growth and learning, rather than as sources of shame or disappointment. It's also important to practice self-care and self-compassion. This means treating yourself with kindness and understanding and recognizing that you are worthy of love and acceptance, flaws, and all. Make time for activities that bring you joy and try to let go of the need for control in your life.

It is essential to understand that perfectionism does not have to define one's identity. A valuable perspective to adopt when exploring oneself is that mistakes are essential and flaws are essential, and that perfectionism does not have to be a part of the equation. Doing so will help break down the barriers that perfectionism creates and foster an environment of personal growth and exploration. Having a more liberal view of personal development and allowing oneself to explore their individual identity without the pressure of being perfect, will lead to a more positive and meaningful experience.

Another important aspect of letting go of perfectionism is to focus on progress, rather than perfection. Rather than striving for perfection in every aspect of your life, try to focus on making small, consistent steps towards your goals. Celebrate your successes, no matter how small they may be, and don't be too hard on yourself when things don't go according to plan. It's important to surround yourself with positive, supportive people. Seek out relationships with individuals who appreciate and accept you for who you are, and who encourage you to be yourself, imperfections, and all. Avoid people who are critical or judgmental and try to distance yourself from toxic relationships that may contribute to your perfectionism.

In conclusion, perfectionism can be incredibly detrimental to one's growth and discovery, as it is not conducive to personal exploration and strives to produce an unrealistic goal. It is important to remember when beginning to discover yourself that you are enough as you are and do not need perfection to be successful or be accepted. It is important to understanding the root of your perfectionism and letting go of perfectionism when building self-worth and self-acceptance. It is important to create a safe environment to allow mistakes and imperfections, as these seemly "weaknesses" are essential to the journey of discovering oneself. With practicing self-compassion and self-care, focusing on progress rather than perfection, and surrounding yourself with positive, supportive people, you can find the freedom and fulfillment you deserve.

Chapter 10

Embracing Your Imperfections

The human being is a beautiful entity, consisting of flaws and imperfections. Our imperfections give us texture and depth that makes us unique and allows us to stand out in a crowd. They make us more interesting, more resilient, and offer certain advantages for our pursuits. Often, the hard times are what help shape us into better people. Therefore, embracing our individual imperfections is essential in both discovering ourselves and finding personal fulfillment. It is said that life is a journey, not a destination. As we discover ourselves, we must seek to embrace our imperfections as part of that journey. It is important to remember that our imperfections, combined with striving for self-improvement and happiness, are the keys to discovering our true selves.

Embracing our imperfections is an important step in building self-worth and self-acceptance. We often feel like we have to be perfect in order to be loved and accepted, but the reality is that no one is perfect. By accepting and embracing our imperfections, we can find freedom from the constant stress and pressure of trying to be perfect, and start to build a more positive, self-compassionate relationship with ourselves.

Letting go of the need for perfectionism is key to embracing our imperfections. We must learn to let go of the pressure to always be perfect, which can be quite difficult. Perfectionism can take a toll on our mental and physical health, as it creates too much internal and external pressure to be perfect. Dedicating too much time to amending perceived flaws can consume our day-to-day life and hinder our growth. Perfectionism is an unrealistic desire that prevents us from realizing our full potential and it is essential to embrace the imperfection and know that makes you are unique.

Steps to Embracing Imperfections

One of the first step in embracing your imperfections is to become aware of them. This means taking a closer look at your thoughts and behaviors and recognizing when you're being overly critical of yourself. Once we let go of the need for perfectionism, we can start to take control of our journey of self-discovery. We can do this by listening to our instincts and following our hearts, as this will lead us to a more fulfilling life. We need to look at our flaws and imperfections as something positive and embrace our own individuality. We must be able to take ownership of all of our traits, turning our weaknesses into strengths and accepting and celebrating them. Try to see your imperfections as opportunities for growth and learning, rather than as sources of shame or disappointment.

Another important aspect of embracing your imperfections is to focus on your strengths and accomplishments. This means celebrating your successes, no matter how small they may be, and focusing on what you do well. Try to view your imperfections as unique qualities that make you who you are and embrace them as part of your individuality. Surrounding yourself with positive, supportive people is very important and make efforts to seek out relationships with individuals who appreciate and accept you for who you are, and who encourage you to be yourself, imperfections, and all. Avoid people who are critical or judgmental and try to distance yourself from toxic relationships that may contribute to your negative self-image.

Next, it's important to practice self-compassion and self-care. This means treating yourself with kindness and understanding and recognizing that you are worthy of love and acceptance, flaws, and all. Make time for activities that bring you joy and try to let go of the need for control in your life. We must practice self-love and compassion and spend time on self-reflection. Only through self-reflection can we become aware of our independent strengths and weaknesses and come to terms with our imperfections. It will also give us an understanding of our needs and a better sense of who we are and what we want in life.

Finally, try to let go of the need for control. This means accepting that there are things in life that we cannot change or control and learning to be comfortable with uncertainty and imperfection. Try to focus on the present moment, and on finding joy and fulfillment in your everyday life.

In conclusion, embracing your imperfections is an essential component of our journey of self-discovery, building self-worth and self-acceptance. By becoming aware of your imperfections, we must learn to let go of perfectionism and accept that our imperfections define and make us unique. Remember to practice self-compassion and self-care, focus on your strengths and accomplishments, surround yourself with positive, supportive people, and let go of the need for control in order to find the fulfillment that you deserve.

Chapter 11

Dealing with Comparison

Growing up in a competitive environment, we are often surrounded by tougher people who could do more than me, who are smarter people than we are, and more beautiful than we are, and the list went on. Comparing ourselves to other people can take away from our own confidence and make us feel like less-than; but it is important to realize that there is a distinction between constructive comparisons and destructive comparisons that can lead to damaging self-criticism if not checked. This chapter addresses how one can reach this sense of liberation through becoming aware of their tendencies for comparison, shifting focus solely on personal goals and achievements, exercising appreciation for what we have rather than resenting others' successes, limiting exposure to social media sources of envy or judgment as well as cultivating positive relationships with uplifting people.

Comparison is a natural human tendency, but it can also be a major hindrance to building self-worth and self-acceptance.

When we compare ourselves to others, we often focus on our perceived shortcomings, which can lead to feelings of insecurity, inadequacy, and low self-esteem. We sometimes compare ourselves to others, whether it's in regard to our appearance, success, or relationships, and this can lead to feelings of inadequacy and low self-worth. Comparison is an unpleasant fact of life that everyone has to face at some point, and it can take a major toll on both our self-worth and acceptance. Unfortunately, it's easier to slip into a pattern of trying to fit in, comparing ourselves to others, and expecting perfection. It's a vicious cycle that can be difficult to break, but it's not impossible. However, it's possible to overcome the negative effects of comparison and build a more positive, self-compassionate relationship with ourselves.

Comparison is an inevitable part of the modern life, with access to social media providing us with a constant source of comparison for our own lives. We are surrounded by images and stories that can make us feel inadequate or envious. It is important that we are mindful of our thoughts and feelings. We should be able to recognize when we are comparing ourselves to someone else and try to focus on our own journey instead. The key is to be gentle and kind to ourselves, instead of judging or criticizing our own actions. Instead of succumbing to these potentially damaging emotions, we can employ strategies such as being mindful of our thoughts and feelings in order to recognize when we may be comparing ourselves to someone else, refusing to judge or criticize ourselves, and actively avoiding sources of comparison like social media. Limit your exposure to social media and other sources of comparison. By doing so we can limit the amount of negative thinking and feelings triggered by comparison pressures on TV and social media platforms.

In your journey for self-discovering and knowing that you are enough, it is important to embrace your own individuality and uniqueness. Recognize that you are valuable and there is no one else in the world exactly like you and recognize that you have your own path to follow and that this is something to be celebrated. Rather than comparing yourself to others, focus on your own goals and aspirations, and what you want to achieve. Embrace your own talents, skills, and strengths, and let go of the need to fit in or conform to societal norms. Developing a strong sense of self-awareness is essential in this process in dealing with comparison. This means being aware of our own thoughts, feelings, and behaviors, and taking the time to reflect on what our strengths and weaknesses are. Identifying our unique skills, qualities, and goals can help us learn to be content with who we really are and what we have to offer. With an open mind and positive perspective, comparison can be seen as an opportunity for growth - something you should use to your advantage when seeking your personal identity without feeling discouraged or belittled.

Practicing gratitude on a regular basis is key for shifting focus away from comparison towards developing an outlook grounded in self-compassion; this helps us to find genuine happiness within ourselves rather than relying upon external sources for validation. Gratitude and self-compassion are two of the most important aspects of living a life of contentment and joy. In an age where comparison is constantly at our fingertips, it can be all too easy to fall into the cycle of comparing yourself to others, disregarding your own growth, progress, and relationships. It is essential to recognize and appreciate the good things in life. Focusing on the positives, instead of always searching for the negatives, can be a powerful tool in taking care of our mental health and well-being. We can acknowledge our success and accomplishments, and even celebrate them. We can also be grateful for what we have and express our appreciation for small blessings, even when faced with challenging situations.

As noted earlier, comparison to others can be a natural and normal part of life, but it is important to keep in mind that each person's journey is unique. Everyone has their own goals and desires, and the focus should always be on their own development above all else. Try to focus on your own goals and aspirations, and work to achieve them, rather than comparing yourself to others. By understanding the uniqueness of one's own life, recognizing its value and setting aspirations for personal growth, people are far more likely to maximize their potential and achieve success than if they judged solely by comparing themselves to those around them. Therefore, fostering an appreciation for one's individuality is essential in order to reach any goal they may have set out for themselves.

Forming meaningful connections and relationships with others can help us combat comparison and build self-worth and acceptance. Connecting with people in our lives who support us and understand us can provide a sense of stability. Supporting and cherishing each other can lead to great life changes, and it's important to remember that everyone has something unique and special to offer.

☐In conclusion, comparison will always be a part of life, but it doesn't have to be a negative force. As much as comparison is inevitable, it is also not impossible to overcome. Everyone has weaknesses, doubts, and insecurities that arise from unfavorable comparisons but with the proper recognition and practices, it is possible to find freedom from comparison and build sustainable self-worth and self-acceptance. By becoming aware of your comparison habits, focusing on your own journey and personal growth, practicing gratitude, limiting our exposure to social media and other sources of comparison, and surrounding yourself with positive, supportive people, we can find freedom from the stress and unhappiness that comparison can bring.

Chapter 12

Practicing Gratitude

Gratitude has been proven to be an important part of discovering your self-worth and self-acceptance. Gratitude is defined as the quality of being thankful and the readiness to show appreciation for and to return kindness. Recognizing the good qualities in oneself has been proven to have positive effects on an individual's physical and emotional wellbeing.

☐One of the most powerful ways to gain self-confidence and overcome feelings of inadequacy and low self-esteem is through expressing gratitude. Many may be surprised to learn that such a simple habit can result in drastic, positive changes in mood and overall well-being. Through appreciation for what we have, we can cultivate greater roundedness in the present moment and develop a strong sense of self-worth.

Those who are able to practice gratitude are less likely to experience negative emotions, such as depression and anxiety, and improved self-acceptance and self-worth. Gratitude helps people discover their self-worth by increasing awareness of their internal capabilities and strengths. They are able to focus on the aspects of themselves that they appreciate, rather than on the traits that make them feel inadequate. One way to practice gratitude is to start a gratitude journal. Each day, write down three things that you're grateful for, no matter how small they may seem. This can be anything from a beautiful sunset to a supportive friend, to a delicious meal. Over time, you'll begin to see the many blessings in your life, and you'll develop a more positive outlook as a result.

Another way to practice gratitude is to actively seek out opportunities to show gratitude and kindness to others. This can be as simple as holding the door open for someone, offering a kind word to a stranger, or volunteering your time to help others. By focusing on the well-being of others, you can shift your focus away from yourself and your own problems and cultivate a sense of gratitude for the good things in your life.

It's also important to be mindful of your thoughts and feelings, and to focus on the positive aspects of your experiences. This means recognizing when you're engaging in negative self-talk, and actively choosing to focus on the good things instead. Over time, this can help you to develop a more positive and self-compassionate outlook, and you'll find it easier to appreciate the good things in your life.

Being aware of and appreciating one's own capabilities, skills and successes helps to cultivate self-confidence. It allows one to feel empowered, knowing that they have the capacity to use their skills and talents to overcome other obstacles. Additionally, by recognizing their own successes, individuals will have a sense of pride and satisfaction in the abilities, rather than feeling insecure and inferior.

Gratitude can also help one to accept their weaknesses, as they become aware and accepting of all of their qualities, regardless of the negative or positive aspects. When they become accepting and appreciative of their weaknesses, they can learn to be gentler and more accepting of themselves, rather than harshly judging their faults and shortcomings. Through cultivating inner acceptance and being thankful for the positive qualities that they possess, individuals can develop a greater sense of self-worth. By focusing on the good things in our lives and recognizing the blessings that we have, we can shift our focus away from comparison and towards a more positive and self-compassionate outlook.

The practice of gratitude can give individuals the necessary self-confidence to persevere through challenges and strive to do better. It can help people to become more in tune with their self-construct and be kinder to themselves when things do not go as planned. Accepting our weaknesses and recognizing our strengths can lead to greater self-worth and ultimately increased self-acceptance. Being thankful allows us to develop a greater sense of worth and acceptance and helps us to understand and appreciate the qualities of ourselves and others around us, rather than fixating on the things that makes us feel inadequate. Gratitude can be the key to greater confidence and self-worth.

Chapter 13

Developing a Growth Mindset

The power of a growth mindset is often understated. A growth mindset is the belief that we can grow and develop as individuals, and that our abilities and intelligence are not fixed. This approach to life is in stark contrast to a fixed mindset, which assumes that our abilities and traits are set in stone and cannot be changed. It provides us with the courage to look within ourselves, reflect on our abilities and traits, and value ourselves in an honest way. By having a growth mindset instead of a fixed one, we are motivated to explore paths we would have otherwise not taken as well as discover aspects of ourselves that build our self-worth and confirm that indeed, we are enough.

Developing a growth mindset can be incredibly empowering, as it helps us to focus on the things that we can control, and to view challenges and setbacks as opportunities for growth and development. Embracing a growth mindset means believing that your skills and talents can be improved through dedication and hard work, and we can break free from limiting beliefs, and tap into our full potential. This positive attitude towards learning and growing allows people to face obstacles without being overwhelmed by them. It emphasizes embracing failure and learning from mistakes as a valuable part of the journey to achieving personal and professional success.

One of the main components of developing a growth mindset is to focus on self-worth and self-acceptance. Research has shown that a person's self-concept and their perceived capabilities have a direct impact on their motivation and overall performance. Consequently, it is important to build self-esteem and recognize personal worth. Consequently, it's important to build self-esteem and recognize personal worth. Self-worth is deeply tied to our beliefs about ourselves.

It's important to recognize personal strengths and capabilities in order to see yourself in a positive light and be constructive in building a strong self-esteem. Knowing that you are capable of tackling a challenge or a hard task is essential for achieving long-term goals. Self-worth is further reinforced by embracing the idea that failure is not an indication of personal failure, but rather an opportunity to learn.

Another way to develop a growth mindset is to practice self-reflection and self-awareness. Take the time to understand your thoughts and emotions, and to identify any limiting beliefs that may be holding you back. Ask yourself questions such as "What are my strengths?" and "What areas can I improve upon?" This type of introspection can help you to gain a deeper understanding of your own abilities and motivations and can be a powerful tool in developing a growth mindset. It is also important is to seek out new experiences and challenges.

Whether it's taking a class in a subject that interests you, volunteering for a new project at work, or trying a new hobby, stepping outside of your comfort zone can help you to develop new skills and grow as a person.

Self-acceptance is equally as crucial in developing a growth mindset. It involves recognizing one's limitations while still committing to the idea that they can continually work to better themselves. It is important to accept yourself, flaws, and all. Understand that no one is perfect and that mistakes are often necessary for growth. It is crucial to embrace failure and setbacks as opportunities for growth, rather than viewing them as personal failures. Recognize that failure is a natural part of the learning and growth process, and that it provides valuable feedback and insights that can help you to improve in the future. Allowing yourself to make mistakes is essential for developing a growth mindset and embracing personal development.

At the end of the day, developing a growth mindset is an essential aspect of building self-worth and self-acceptance that assures that we are enough. By focusing on the things that you can control, seeking out new experiences and challenges, practicing self-reflection and self-awareness, cultivating a positive attitude, and embracing failure and setbacks as opportunities for growth, you can tap into your full potential and live a more fulfilling and meaningful life. Therefore, remaining patient yet diligent will ultimately lead to improved performance and greater overall satisfaction with life. With this in mind, developing a growth mindset becomes attainable through increasing self-worth and self-acceptance.

Chapter 14

Cultivating Self-Care

The concept of self-care is one that promotes personal wellbeing and holistic development for individuals. It includes anything from taking time for yourself to practicing good physical, emotional health, and mental well-being, and engaging in activities that bring us joy and fulfillment. Self-care is part of maintaining healthy lifestyle and it is important to have healthy habits to prevent illness and promote well-being.

It is beneficial to take some time out for yourself each day to relax and rejuvenate in your journey to self-discovery and knowing that we are enough. While self-care can take many forms, it is essential to recognize the relationship between self-care and self-worth and self-acceptance. Cultivating meaningful self-care activities can help individuals gain a better sense of self and improve their overall quality of life.

In the journey of discovering yourself and knowing that you are enough, self-worth is an individual's evaluation of their own value, esteem, and worthiness. A core belief of self-worth is that everyone is equal and deserves respect and dignity. With this in mind, it is important to practice meaningful self-care in order to provide yourself with a foundation for self-esteem. Self-care offers individuals an opportunity to take time for themselves and their own needs. Taking time to relax, recognize accomplishments and nurture our physical, emotional, and spiritual well-being helps us to recognize that we are capable and worthy of respect.

Similarly, self-acceptance involves the understanding and acceptance of the qualities that make us who we are. It is not just about accepting the good, but also the bad and embracing them equally. As with self-esteem, self-acceptance can be fostered through meaningful self-care. Cultivating self-care can help individuals become more connected to their own bodies, feelings, and emotions. Taking the time to practice self-care reinforces the understanding of oneself and provides us with the opportunity to reflect and come to terms with our own unique characteristics.

The first step to cultivating self-care is to identify your own needs and wants. This could involve taking an inventory of your physical, emotional, and mental well-being, and identifying areas where you would like to make improvements. It's important to be honest with yourself, and to recognize that everyone's needs are different. It's important to recognize that self-care is not a one-time event, but a lifelong journey. By staying committed to your personal growth and well-being, you can continue to develop your self-care skills, and tap into your full potential.

Once you have a clear understanding of your own needs, the next step is to develop a self-care plan. This could involve setting achievable goals, such as engaging in regular exercise, eating a balanced diet, or getting enough sleep. It may also involve incorporating mindfulness and meditation into your daily routine, or taking up a new hobby that brings you joy and fulfillment. It's also important to make self-care a priority, and to carve out time for it in your busy schedule. This could involve setting aside a specific time each day for self-care activities or making it a priority to engage in self-care activities on a regular basis.

In addition to these self-care activities, it's also important to practice self-compassion. This means treating ourselves with kindness and understanding and recognizing that we are all doing the best that we can. Self-compassion can help us to reduce feelings of stress and anxiety, and to develop greater resilience in the face of life's challenges.

Overall, cultivating meaningful self-care activities is essential for creating a foundation of self-respect, self-worth, and self-acceptance. Self-care helps individuals to recognize their own inherent worth and capabilities and gain clearer insight into who they are. Whether it is taking time to practice relaxation, mindfulness or physical activity, self-care does not have to be time-consuming or require a lot of money – it only requires taking time for oneself. With the emphasis on self-care, individuals can start to build a sense of self-respect and appreciation, setting them on the path to a life of acceptance and wellbeing.

Chapter 15

Living Your Best Life

Life is a journey filled with experiences and lessons, but one of the most important aspects of attaining joy throughout our lives is discovering our self-worth. Living your best life is about embracing your authentic self, embracing your strengths and weaknesses, and living in alignment with your values and beliefs.

Discovering yourself and knowing that you are enough is about living a life that is fulfilling, meaningful, and satisfying. Knowing our self-worth while discovering our self and knowing that we are enough lays the foundation for reaching our highest potential, allowing us to live happily and fulfill ourselves. This means embracing your strengths and weaknesses, and recognizing that you are enough, just as you are.

It is important to know that without understanding your true worth, you won't be able to develop meaningfully in life or create joy that will last through every trial and tribulation we may face. By developing self-worth, you can reduce feelings of anxiety and insecurity, and feel more confident and empowered in our daily life. In short, discovering your self-worth is the path to a living life to our highest potential.

The first step in living your best life is to identify your core values and beliefs. This will help you to understand what is truly important to you, and what you want to prioritize in your life. Once you have a clear understanding of your values and beliefs, you can start to align your life with these principles. Another key component of living your best life is to develop a strong sense of self-worth. This means embracing your strengths and weaknesses, and recognizing that you are enough, just as you are. By developing self-worth, you can reduce feelings of anxiety and insecurity, and feel more confident and empowered in your daily life.

Another step to discovering your self-worth is taking responsibility. It is important to acknowledge that while life can be challenging, it is also up to each individual to make their own decisions and strive to make the most of whatever opportunities are available. Taking ownership and being accountable for one's actions is a surefire way to build self-confidence, paving the way for greater self-worth.

In order to live your best life, it is also important to challenge yourself. It is essential to set goals and don't be afraid to take risks. By pushing yourself, you are able to evaluate which ideas and projects you feel most passionate about and can determine a course of action to pursue them. This process naturally increases your sense of self-worth because it enables you to discover what you are capable of achieving.

Setting boundaries is another important component of living your best life. This means setting limits and expectations for your relationships, work, and other areas of your life. By setting boundaries, you can protect your time, energy, and resources, and ensure that you are living in alignment with your values and beliefs.

Embracing a growth mindset is also critical to living your best life. This means recognizing that growth is a lifelong process, and that you are capable of developing new skills and abilities throughout your life. By embracing a growth mindset, you can approach challenges with a positive and proactive attitude and continue to grow and evolve over time.

Perhaps the most important element of living your best life while discovering your self-worth is engaging in meaningful relationships. Surrounding yourself with supportive and understanding people can help cultivate a healthier relationship with yourself and also provide much-needed encouragement and guidance. Additionally, being involved in activities that bring nonprofit organizations and communities together can open up doors of self-discovery. Being of service and giving back to others can be an incredibly enriching experience and can unlock many new aspects of one's character.

Cultivating a sense of gratitude is another major step in living our best life. This means focusing on the things that you are thankful for, and recognizing the blessings in your life, even in the midst of adversity. By embracing gratitude, you can increase feelings of happiness, joy, and well-being, and experience more fulfillment in your life.

And finally, living our best life is about embracing your authentic self, embracing your strengths and weaknesses, and living in alignment with your values and beliefs. By developing self-worth, setting boundaries, embracing a growth mindset, and cultivating gratitude, you can live a life that is fulfilling, meaningful, and satisfying. Living your best life and discovering your self-worth is an ongoing process, but one that is well worth the journey. The rewards of greater self-confidence, enhanced self-worth, and a life of purpose and fulfillment will be worth all of the effort. By taking ownership of one's life, pushing past comfort zones, and developing meaningful relationships, one can pursue their highest level of being.

In conclusion, this book has provided a comprehensive guide to discovering your self-worth and living your best life while knowing that you are enough. Through exploring your thoughts, emotions, values, and beliefs, you have been encouraged to embrace your authentic self and develop a strong sense of self-worth. You have learned about overcoming negative self-talk, accepting, and loving yourself, building confidence, finding your purpose, setting boundaries, letting go of perfectionism, embracing imperfections, dealing with comparison, practicing gratitude, developing a growth mindset, and cultivating self-care. By following the advice and strategies outlined in this book, you have the tools you need to live a life that is fulfilling, meaningful, and satisfying. You can live with purpose and passion, in alignment with your values and beliefs, and with a strong sense of self-worth and self-confidence.

Remember, the journey towards discovering your self-worth, knowing you are enough and living your best life is ongoing and will continue throughout our lifetime. But with dedication, commitment, and perseverance, you can develop the skills, habits, and attitudes that will help you to live a life that is truly meaningful and fulfilling. Having self-worth and an understanding that you are enough is the key to having a life full of joy and fulfillment, attainable and necessary in order to reach your highest potential; through self-reflection and personal exploration, one can unlock and embrace your worth for a path of success as well as lasting jubilation. Know that you are definitely enough. Be blessed.

Printed in Great Britain
by Amazon